MENTAL NURTURING

FROM 0 TO 5 AND BEYOND

JERRY COOK

Copyright © 2021 by Jerry Cook.

All rights reserved. No part of this book may be reproduced in any written, electronic, recording, or photocopying without written permission of the publisher or author. The exception would be in the case of brief quotations embodied in articles or reviews and pages where permission is specifically granted by the publisher or author.

Jerry Cook/Mental Nurturing
Printed in the United States of America

Although every precaution has been taken to verify the accuracy of the information contained herein, the author and publisher assume no responsibility for any errors or omissions. No liability is assumed for damages that may result from the use of information contained within.

Mental Nurturing/ Jerry Cook -- 1st ed.

CONTENTS

Introduction 1
Chapter 1 9
Chapter 2 13
Chapter 3 21
Chapter 4 25
Chapter 5 29
Chapter 6 33
Chapter 7 37
Chapter 8 43
Chapter 9 47
Chapter 10 53
Chapter 11 57
Chapter 12 61
Chapter 13 69
Chapter 14 75
Conclusion 79

I dedicate this book to my deceased mother, who was my rock for the first 17 years of my life.

Mom, you made me go to Sunday school every Sunday morning. You used a switch to discipline me, but you took the time and had the wisdom to instruct me as to why you used that switch. You gave me an excellent foundation for life.

I wandered off, Mom, but I came back because of the foundation you gave me for the first 17 years of my life. I was not allowed to attend your funeral, but I cried, and chose to remember the good times I had with you. I think about you all the time. I love you, and you can be proud of me, too. You raised a good son, Mom.

I want to acknowledge the most instrumental people in my life: Crystal, Chanel, Jerry, and Johnathan, my wonderful four children. That's my family. They have always shown me love and concern. I'm happy to be their father.

To my eight grandchildren, I love you all. And to all my relatives thank you for your support as well. .

And lastly, I want to acknowledge a true follower of Jesus. If I had not met pastor Jacob Crawford, this book would not have been written. He called me one day and said that he wanted to interview me. As a result of that interview, this book was initiated. He helped me immeasurable with the process.

INTRODUCTION

My name is Jerry Cook, the author of this book. I wrote this book because God commissioned me to write it. I am 77 years old. I was born in a very small town in Mississippi in 1943. My family consisted of eight siblings, four boys and four girls.

Regardless of your natural origin, race, creed, or color, if you read this book, you will see life with a different prospective than you have right now. You should be capable realizing that human beings' conduct and character have changed much more than the climate and season changes that we are witnessing now. This change will be the main purpose of the book.

This is a book that the masses in society need to read. It is the message I keep getting from God our Creator. Its contents may expose matters and circumstances that involve any given race. If the shoe fits, wear it.

I have procrastinated in putting this book to print. It is filled with wisdom that God blessed me with during the 31 years I was incarcerated in a Louisiana State Prison, which is named Angola, for the crime of arm robbery.

In my first ten years at Angola, God revealed a multitude of things to me about life—sometimes while I was sitting in my cell and at other times when I was out of my cell in the yard. God also revealed to me things about the society I once lived in—a society that would grow in the exacerbation in conduct and character. I said to myself, how could they let this happen?

When I was released from prison, I found a society that was much worse than I envisioned in prison.

My father was uneducated, and he was not what society would call a good role model. He drank a lot, cursed a lot, but he was a hard worker, and he tried to provide money to keep food on our table: however, he spent some of the money working on alcohol, but overall, he was not a bad man.

My mother was highly intelligent for having only a 4th grade education and was a brilliant woman in my eyesight. She instilled principles, values, morals, love, and spirituality into my countenance over the 17 years. I have cried many tears for the sorrow I may have caused her after I left home at 17 years old.

I joined the U.S. Army when I was 17 years old. My mother had to sign papers for me to enlist. I passed to the 11th grade when I enlisted in the Army. I attained a GED within my first year in the Army. I was an honor roll student throughout all my years attending public school.

My Army experience was bittersweet. I was a good soldier regarding carrying out my military duties, however it was because of my off-duty activities that led me to receive a bad conduct discharge. My job for most of my military experience was that of the company commander's driver and radio operator, which was at that time a prestigious job for a soldier to have. I got the job as company commander's driver because I stayed neat perpetually, spit shined boots and all. I earned the job because of my persona, and I knew how to operate radio equipment, and I was a quick study with the phonetic codes and the best operator in my company.

My second prison term was in LCIS, a Louisiana at a satellite prison located in Dequincy, LA, of which I served 5 ½ years on a manslaughter guilty plea. I learned a lot during those 5 ½ years. I became more humane in thought and spirit, but my mind was not capable of purposeful focus.

Then came my last incarcerated state, which I endured for 31 continuous years. The incarcerated state that God converted me to be the man I am today. I would like to think that I am a modern day "Paul" who was called by God on the Damascus Road.

I was sentenced to 198 years for 2 armed robberies, which was to me a very austere sentence because in the armed robberies, considering no one was hurt.

My greatest burden to bear in prison was the fact that I left 4 children in society. I cried many nights because I could not be there for them in the physical sense.

However, God put it in my mind to be involved with my children through the written page from prison. God blessed me with wisdom to maintain my parental concerns and with love, in spite of my incarceration. I have 4 children (2 boys and 2 girls) and 8 grandkids. I maintained fatherhood by writing them all regular letters throughout my incarceration; however, the first 10 years of my incarnation were the most profound and tumultuous years of incarnation. I wrote them more in those years because being lock away in isolation provided more time to reflect on being the best parent I could be, despite my incarceration. We all embrace a wonderful love relationship. My sons are great fathers to their children, and my daughter is a wonderful mother to her children. All our family attend church and are rooted in spirituality. By the grace of God, we are all bonded in love as a family.

After my first 10 years of incarceration, God blessed me to become a literacy instructor. I was approached by the Classification Officer who has a station in the inmate kitchen (Chow Hall) , so an inmate that wants to speak with him about a job or issue could approach him before the inmate left the Chow Hall to go back to the dorm.

On the day in question, I was walking in line with my peers in the Chow Hall, and a Classification Officer) called out to me. "Hey, Cook! You want a job as a tutor"? My first thought after hearing this offer was one of doubt and surprise. In previous years, I had not had good relationship with the security nor any prison official. Which is the reason why I was shocked at being offered a job as a tutor or any other job..

I didn't quite know how to respond, so I told him, "Man, you all leave me alone. I am trying to back up from conflict with y'all." (For the first 10 years in Angola Prison I was given over 110 disciplinary write ups. I was put out of every camp located in Angola. I was put out because I perpetually filed administrative remedy procedures and lawsuits. I wrote to federal judges that oversaw consent decrees. As well as, governors, senators, and the president complaining about the treatment and conditions in Angola Prison. No camp officials wanted me in their camp.) The Classification

Officer responded to me: "No! No! No! Do you want a job as a tutor? I'm not messing with you!" With that effusive reply, he got my sincere attention. God directed my mind to a conversation I had with my oldest daughter when she came to visit me at the worst punishment camp in Angola. The camp was called "Camp J." When security brought me out of my cell to the visiting area to see my daughter, I was in cuffs on both my hands and feet. She had visited me numerous times over a ten-year span, but she had never seen me in shackles and hands and feet. Her instant action was to audibly cry real tears. Her reaction stuck me in the heart and hurt and shame filled my human spirit. I shed a tear myself.

My daughter and I proceeded to visit even under this condition and circumstances. At

the conclusion of our visit, I made my daughter a promise. I told her, "You will never see me like this again, and I promise you that." That promise I gave my daughter was the catalyst to my conversion in Angola Prison. That promise I gave her compelled me to see a way to fulfill it by becoming a tutor in Angola instead of being an antagonist.

So, when I answered, I did so indignantly. "Yeah! Yeah! Yeah! I want a tutor job." The classification officer told me to come to his office when finished eating, and he would give me a test, and if I passed the test, he would give me a job. I complied with his instructions and went to his office.

I was amazed at the test (20 words on a standard piece of paper). He knew I could read those words because I wrote several administrative remedy procedures against conditions and treatment over the years for which he had to answer.

I zipped through the 20 words with rapidity, and after passing the menial test that a 6 grader could pass, , he logically said, "You passed the test," and he directed me on matters for the first day that I would begin tutoring.

Through this process, I gained a lot of wisdom as I carried out my responsibility as a tutor. I started as a literacy tutor primarily teaching how to read, write and basic math. I graduated to a GED Tutor which gets students to the level where they can obtain a high school diploma equivalency. Through my stages of development in prison, God guided my steps in preparation for the writing of this book. I'm writing this book like the biblical figure "Paul" wrote epistles in the New Testament.

God is not pleased with the human reactions we are engaging. God wants us to care, share, love, and be concerned about the welfare of each other. This is how God wants mankind to live.

To the billionaires and millionaires, the very country and its liberties that allowed you to become who you are needs your attention and support. When democracy falls so will the safeguards you've enjoyed in becoming who you are will disappear. If this great nation falls, your new currency and personal wealth will cease to be. I have further dialogue for the rich in this book.

Men of little wisdom have limited vision. The wealthy men that support and are engaged in the failure of the very democracy that made him/her rich are in essence fighting the success they now enjoy.

God wants the rich to give to the nation that blessed them to be rich. The time is now, and the time is urgent.

So, my first ten years God worked on me, and in the final 21 years, God worked through me. I not only taught literacy and GED classes, but I also taught parenting classes. By God's grace, I was chosen to be the first prisoner to teach parenting classes to Angola harden criminals.

Security and administrators obviously knew of my constant letters to all my children because inmates mail is not confidential. Just like they knew I was qualified to be a tutor, they also knew that I would and could teach incongruous men how to be better fathers even from prison by teaching them parenting classes.

It was a difficult task at first, because most prisoners did not want to participate. This was a program compelled for inmates that had only 6 months left in prison; however, but by God's grace, it became very easy to do after only a few sessions. After the first class, I put together a graduation banquet for the participants at the end of the parenting class period. The banquet consisted of a full course dinner and entertainment. This was a motivation for other prisoners to willing participate in the program.

As a result of these classes, another parent related group named "Malachi Dads" came into existence. Once a year, fathers could spend a day with his children with liberties to engage in games and other social activities. I know for a fact that better fathers went back to their children as a result of participating in these programs because I see some of them from time to time out here in free society, and they all have a wonderful relationship with their children.

A satellite Bible college was established in Angola. I attended that Bible college for the last 4 years of my incarceration and attained an associate and bachelor's degree with a 3.5 GPA. The Bible college experience was enlightening and informative, my spiritual insight was greatly enhanced.

I was released from prison when I competed my final semester in the Bible college in 2012. I believe that it was God's divine guidance that made my release happen that way.

I have provided a brief chronological order of my life's journey with the hope and expectation that you will in fact read the book that God incited me to give to the masses in our society. I am a firm believer that God works in mysterious ways with wonders to perform.

God preserved my life when I became incarcerated and watched over me throughout my incarceration preparing me to write this book. God made me a new man. A man with compassion and wisdom as opposed to being vicious and revengeful.

God gave us a beautiful world to live in. To keep it that way, there are things we need to do to keep it that way. This message is for all of humanity. Please read this book.

I dedicate this book to my 4 children, 8 grandchildren, 5 in-laws, my brother and 3 sisters, all my other relatives and friends, and humanity.

I do not want to merely talk about Jesus. I want to live like Jesus in my heart and deeds.

CHAPTER 1

Functional Insanity (You Can Make a Difference)

I've read books that expounded on how many times successful people failed before they succeeded. The most outstanding story I read about people failing time and time again was in the book entitled *Think and Grow Rich* authored by Napoleon Hill. In this book, Mr. Hill stated that Thomas Edison failed time and time again trying to invent the electric light; he said that people thought Edison was insane as he kept trying to make light come from what was in the air. As we can all witness today, Thomas Edison invented the electric light.

Omnifarious manifestations that we enjoy today came from one man's invention. What kind of world would this be if one man Thomas Edison had not been persistent in believing in himself and what he believed could be? If we as individuals, adopt Thomas Edison's resolve and refuse to let failure stop us in trying to fulfill our aspirations and dreams. You will succeed, Thomas Edison failed over a thousand times before he finally succeeded to invent the electric light. Edison had faith that he could make a difference. Do you?

Let me try to simplify my assertion by looking at contemporary society. I personally feel that most people's brain usage can be verified by looking at academic achievements. For example, most high school graduates get better pay than school dropouts. College graduates and people with doctoral degrees usually get paid more than people with lesser degrees. Let's apply common sense here. High school students who graduate store more knowledge in their brain learned from books; college students store more knowledge in their brain because of the advanced studies they take after high school; and the same applies to the various degrees attain by whomever. The more you put in the more you get out.

Some people attain good paying jobs without finishing high school or ever going to college. (There are exceptions to every rule.) Some people are gifted with specialized skills and or trades, and some people will use examples of a person they know who makes lots of money but never went to college. People that use the example I spoke of are not using common sense, reason, logic, nor practicality properly because they fail to equate the number of people making it without going to college to the number of people making it who did go to college.

The truth is that most people making lots of money are indeed the ones who went to college and in essence stored knowledge in their brain. So which way would you go: the way of the majority or the way of minority? The world has changed a lot, but one thing remains consistent, and that is there will always be a best or worse in every aspect of life. The one you choose will determine your future. The best minds are the ones filled with knowledge and schooling provides knowledge to the brain.

The bottom line is your opportunity to make lots of money is to fill your brain with book knowledge that you can turn into cash after schooling.

As an individual, you have a vested interest in making this world a better place because you are in fact a part of this world. You are one of the over seven billion people who make up the world's population, and you can make a difference in the world. You can be the next Thomas Edison to the world.

If you think you can't do anything about anything, you fight yourself. Most people who feel that they can't do anything about whatever fight themselves by letting that thought keep them from trying.

You, an individual within the masses, have a right and responsibility to join in with the rest of the world to make it better. Do not let anyone discourage from doing what you really want to do. Some people will allow what a friend or others have to say about a given thing persuade them to think how they think. What happens to your brain when you follow what comes from other brains?

You will find yourself always trying to see what others think about matters before you make a decision, and eventually, your ability to think independently will dissipate. You will become what I term in this book as "functionally Insane". Millions of Americans fall into the trap of not thinking individually.

As an individual, you are your best friend, literally, and most people haven't thought of it as a fact, even though we all heard the old cliché that states "a man is his own best friend and worst enemy." I'm not certain about a man being his own enemy.

When you ask someone who their best friend is, they begin to immediately start thinking of someone other than themselves. People will start naming those thought to be friends, never even considering everything they thought a best friend should be to them they are that themselves to themselves.

Let's take inventory. From the moment you wake up, don't you start talking to your best friend mentally and sometimes vocally? When you have a decision to make don't you talk it over with yourself first? Even the decision to call or go see a best friend, you discuss with yourself first whether to do it. You should trust in yourself more as an individual now that you know who your best friend really is.

Regarding the worst enemy, I think I will have to go along with that part, too. The bad decisions you make is a good example of your being your own worst enemy. Any negativity that you engage in coming from your worst enemy.

Your best friend and worst enemy battle for supremacy in your brain. If you train your best friend to dominate and control your brain. You will never invite the thought, "I'm just one person, and I can't do anything" thoughts to enter your mind. For 31 years, I endured perpetual incarceration while watching the country I love slip into a place I couldn't recognize.

I am writing this book to hopefully, by the grace of God, save this country from self-destruction. Our society has been blinded. Perhaps the reason for this blindness is ignorance or the inability to use common sense, reason, logic, and practicality. This lack of common sense, reason, logic, and practicality can be traced all the way back to birth. Therefore, I want to begin this book by expounding on human development that takes place from ages 0 to 5.

CHAPTER 2

Since the beginning of time, we as humans have overlooked the crucial years of human development. Mental development and nurturing can be considered the keys that unlock the door to life's endeavors. We must carefully develop a plan of how we will develop the human mind of children from 0 to 5 years of age. Parents must be reminded that they are the first real teachers of these children. It has been assumed that every woman who has a baby knows how to take care of and teach her baby. This is not the case. Training is needed. Mental nurturing of children from 0 to 5 years old is foundational for life. It is believed that 90% of the human brain is fully developed by age 5. It is critical that young children have a solid foundation, just like newly built homes. As a matter of fact, unrelated to the building of a house, all living things require special attention in early development.

All produce raised for human consumption is raised with special attention. All the crops in our fields need special attention in cultivation and nurturing. Malnourished animals cannot be brought to market. Vegetables and other field crops cannot bear good harvest if not cultivated and nurtured. How could we, as a society, expect children from 0 to 5 years of age to have a foundation for life without proper mental nurturing?

If a child is born into an environment that is filled with perpetual cursing, fighting between family members, selfishness, hunger, stealing and other negative behaviors, then such behaviors will be viewed as normal. When a child goes off to school, they will display these characteristics and behaviors in classrooms. Often, these same children are placed on medications for ADHD, when the real diagnosis should be "bad parenting."

Children who fail to get proper mental nurturing are likely to live an unproductive life at no fault of their own. County and state prisons are filled with men and women who had little positive mental nurturing from 0 to 5 years of age. What I've notice from my prison teaching experience, is that many of my student displayed negative characteristic they picked up in earlier years. Those who go in and out of prison are never given a chance from birth. Is it right to punish a human for being born? The answer is no. Yet, we do so through our courts of law when the real problem is a lack of mental nurturing by one's parents.

The courts fail when they prosecute a person for committing a crime without considering the person's mental nurturing. Many people argue that when humans reach a certain age (no matter how they were raised), a person will know right from wrong. Therefore, the people who are committing crimes are doing so because they want to. I want people to realize that these teenage boys and girls, as well as grown adults, are doing the wrong things simply because they have been mentally nurtured with flagitious activity. For example, why do millions of people smoke regular cigarettes when they know smoking cigarettes is bad for their health and could eventually kill them? People won't give up smoking because it becomes a habit. It is all they know. The same is true of the behavior of children. They mimic what they see and experience. Just as smoking cigarettes provides comfort for the smoker, so does wrongdoing provide normalcy for the child. Many troubled adults only know wrongdoing, and they lack the job skills needed for success. So, when you look at adults and wonder why they do the things they do, consider what kind of mental nurturing they received from 0 to 5.

To my knowledge, no programs have been designed to ensure that every child gets proper mental nurturing from 0 to 5 effectively. There are some programs that exist but the effectiveness is subject. I view this oversight as something that needs to be urgently addressed. No child asks to be born. I believe each child that is born deserves a chance to live a decent life. The only way we fix this as a society is to work together to design programs to ensure that every child born is nurtured properly at home.

Most people in society do not really know why two-year-olds do what they do. Two-year-olds have been given the stigma of "terrible twos." Most people will make statements like "those are some bad little rascals," "they are hardheaded," or "they don't do anything you ask them." Most of society does not really understand why two-year-old's act as they do because they have never picked up a parenting book. Further, they have not given any intense thought about why two-year-olds act the way that they do. Little attention has been directed to teaching society about the characteristics of children from 0 to 5. As a result, many children suffer from child abuse and neglect, when they are only trying to find out how to live and doing things that are natural in human development.

Two-year-olds act the way they do because at the age of two they realize they are human after two years of observing, and observation turns into recognition. The beginning stage in human development is observation. From birth, a baby can only observe the people in their environment. They have little understanding. It's a strange and new situation they have been thrust into. After continual observation, the child begins to store information into their brain (mental development) at a greater degree, and they begin to recognize faces, sounds, and objects. As the child grows and matures, he or she learns more and more from observation.

When a child engages in physical movement, he or she is inadvertently filling the brain with more knowledge concerning physicality. This includes the raising of the head, push up from the arms, rolling over and so forth. Before a child reaches two years of age, he or she is dependent upon someone else to do things for them. Often in the process, the child might have to cry, throw a tantrum, or throw something to get attention and to get what they want. Beginning at age two, children go through a stage in human development called "independence."

Two-year-old's have gone through the process of observation and reached the stage of human recognition and identification. At two years of age, a child sees that he or she can do stuff without anyone's help. The child recognizes that he or she is human just like everyone else. In this stage of independence, a child thinks that he or she can do whatever everyone else around them can do. A child often thinks that he or she is "big stuff" upon the realization of their humanity. This leads to daring behavior patterns.

A two-year-old going through this stage is fearless, adventurous, prideful, a know-it-all, and independent.

Parenting is critical. Parents must provide the new adventurer proper guidance on how to navigate through life. A two-year-old must be taught and not abused by an angry parent who sees the child's actions as disobedient. Parents should be taught to never strike a two-year-old out of anger. Parents should be taught to recognize the beauty of a two-year-old being mischievous and embrace their child's curiosity. Parents should use their child's curiosity as an opportunity to teach their child right from wrong. A parent must understand that proper communication with a child is very important. They must be reminded that a two-year-old's brain is not fully developed, and the child cannot discern right from wrong or make good decisions at that age; they just think that they can.

We must replace the stigma of "terrible twos" with accurate facts that explain why children act as they do. Two-year-olds hear what is being said about them and often fulfill those negative expectations. This has a negative effect on the child. Children will often act out so that they will receive attention from their parents.

Everyone born deserves to have the opportunity to live a decent life. The years 0 to 5 are crucial in human development. Mental nurturing is the main focus in the development of humans. It is long past time to concentrate on the mental nurturing of our newborns and children.

Children who are physically and mentally nurtured are less likely to engage in criminal behavior. We, as a society, should be concerned, but unfortunately, too many are not. Little has been done to ensure that children are born into positive environments that include proper mental and physical nurturing. Children are often birthed by precocious mothers and have no father figure. We observe these trends and have much to say, but we do little or nothing as a society to address the problem.

I believe that any female who happens to become impregnated with a child should be mandated to attend a program that highlights the developmental characteristics of newborns and children (especially ages 0 to 5 years). Hopefully, in this process, the mother will be taught to embrace a love for the new life inside of her. Not all women who have babies really want to be mothers. Women having babies might need to be influenced to love the baby through empathy or sympathy. Empathy can be invoked by reminding the mother that when she looks at the child, she sees herself in that child and that the child needs her love and affection to survive. Sympathy can be invoked by trying to get her to understand that this child did not ask to be born. This child should not have to be raised by someone else. All women having babies should be persuaded by their humanity.

Pregnant teens at a precocious age are in of need specialized programs designed to ensure that they know how to mentally nurture the new life that they are now responsible for. Their role is not only to mother but also to be the teacher. It is important for them to know that they are their child's first teacher.

Facilities need to be established for new mothers that provide guidance. Some mothers may struggle to find their way and may need help to get back on track. The facilities need to be partnered with doctors, social workers, and mental health specialists.

Parenting classes should be a mandated fixture at these facilities. Only with these types of facilities can we assure that every child will get a fair chance to be properly nurtured for life.

CHAPTER 3

Awareness of "mental nurturing" can reverse the conduct and character of America. Every action that is or ever was began with a thought in someone's mind. The best way to find a solution is to start with the source. If that sounds logical and reasonable, then perhaps you will agree with me that 0 to 5 is an excellent place to begin. If we can influence what goes into the brains of our youngest children, then it will be an inevitable change in the future action of our society. Children grow up to be flawed adults without proper mental nurturing from 0 to 5 years.

Have you ever seen a child in a hopeless situation? If not, then you need to visit some of the many low-income neighborhoods, projects, or even public areas where children play. I implore those who are rich to ride a city bus through a low-income area, walk through a project, or low-income housing area. If you are humane, you will feel the pain that so many innocent children go through, and you will comprehend why these children act the way they do. Children cannot pick their parents. The ones subject to hopelessness cannot do anything about it, but our society must do something.

Many youths who drop out of school do so because of a lack of mental nurturing. I am appalled at how we have allowed our public schools to be exploited rather than educate our children. I cannot believe that adults cannot control the conduct and character of the children in school. That said, teachers cannot change a student's negative behavior patterns that are constantly reinforced at home. A schoolteacher was once the third or surrogate parent to students. The student was assigned to a teacher. In my opinion, too many of the public-school teachers are not qualified to proficiently teach the academic subjects they attempt to teach. All teachers should be certified and equitably paid. It would be reasonable to assess that any public-school teacher that cannot control the conduct in a classroom could never fulfill the role of a surrogate parent.

Since schools were integrated, there has been a constant decline in public school funding. The government has consistently revoked or cut public school funding. I'm not an expert on the many designs that has been used, but I do know that most public schools have been so exacerbated that many children dread going to school instead of showing an eagerness to learn. They dread going because of a variety of reasons: noise in the classrooms, the teacher is an inept instructor, or bullying.

Common sense is disappearing from our society. This implies that the intelligence of society at large has declined. Intelligence is obtained largely through reading at a young age. A lack of educational achievement results in ignorance. Many of our public schools' graduate boys and girls who can barely read or write. Students are passed from grade to grade just so the teachers can get them out of their class. That is not only shameful, but it is also detrimental to our free society. By graduating young men and women with little or no education, we are creating an unintelligent society. This problem is manifesting in adults that are not equipped to use common sense, much less, compete with others in the job market. These unequipped young men and women are destined to failure.

If you take a chunk of intelligence out of your society, don't you think it would cause a societal change? Do you think there is no harm in letting public school decline? Our society must face the facts. Because our schools are allowed to fail the conduct and character of our society exacerbates with every passing year, our prisons and jails are warehouses for the uneducated.

The greater portion of people who are incarcerated are people with little to no education. Criminologists all over the world have confirmed that the more education a person has, the less likely that he or she will commit a crime. Who can believe that we want to stop crime in our nation when we allow the most effective tool that prevents criminal endeavors to decline in effectiveness and method? How can we say we want to help our young men and women yet stand idly by and witness a school system that graduates young people who can barely read or write?

CHAPTER 4

The Functional Insanity of Government

Campaign finance reform must become a reality. A senate race can cost millions of dollars, yet the salary for this office only pays $174,000 annually. This is unreasonable, illogical, lacking common sense, and certainly impractical. Can you now envision how "functional insanity" is at play here? Do you think we have a mental problem? Please think of the poor children you could have helped by putting clothes on their back or shoes on their feet with the money you gave for political purposes. You are giving money to a government official who will already be paid by your tax dollars.

I believe that those highly educated men in congress can easily solve this problem. However, we must demand that those we elect do their job and pass campaign finance reform. This reform will put integrity, dignity, and fairness back into our elections. As United States citizens, we need not ask but demand that our congressmen pass real campaign reform laws. This includes limitations on the amount of money that corporate America and private citizens can give to political causes. Our nation will continue to decline and self-destruct if we do not act.

Another example of the functional insanity of government is congress' political monopoly. Many senators and representatives join "the club" once they get to Washington D.C. They join the "you scratch my back and I'll scratch yours" club. They say, "You vote with me on this, and I'll vote with you on that"—not realizing that they are compromising their integrity and damaging their character. There should be a term limit for congressmen. Politics was never meant to be a profession. I truly believe that men in the congressional halls would be more conscious about doing the job at hand. Term limits would weed out those who were serving for selfish purposes, or for the purpose of making a career out of being a representative or senator. Elected office is not supposed to be a career but an intention to serve your country's needs.

I have some questions for our congressional leaders: Have you ever ridden on a public bus? Have you ever walked down the street of a low-income area or sat in a low-income playground? If you haven't, then I encourage you to do so. Millions of our citizens live in these environments. How can you represent people that you do not know or understand? Congressional leaders rarely, if ever, go into low-income areas. Year after year, congressional leaders get a salary to be the voice of all the people, yet they do not know what people need because they seldom take the time to go where the poor live. Experience is the best teacher.

Senators and representatives only work for six months. It would be beneficial for those leaders to spend the other six months in their communities, getting to know all the people—rich and poor. Imagine the solutions that could developed to help those most marginalized. What kind of example do our congressional leaders provide for our society, especially our children? Are they helping or hurting the "mental nurturing" of our societal masses?

Congressmen and congresswomen should set better examples and work twelve months a year like everyone else. They get paid much more money than the average worker, and they are privileged to enormous fringe benefits. Six months of exposure in the communities could result in more empathy. Congress is a contributor to the imperfections that are exacerbating our democratic experience. In our early years of life, we depend upon our parents, and in the later years, we depend upon the people we elect. I would ask every public servant to look into his or her heart with real truthfulness, and ask, "Am I doing the best I can to serve the people who pay my salary?" The moral consciousness of elected officials needs a revival. Each representative and senator seemingly look at their jobs as a career instead of an opportunity to serve our nation's masses. They desire to do only the things that will increase their possibilities to get reelected. Once in office, reelection is their main focus and affects how they do their job.

Elected officials who vote on matters in a way to get reelected should be called out and rejected by their voters that put him or her in office. The only elected officials who deserve to be reelected are the ones who maintain integrity and voted their consciousness on all matters.

We as Americans have a responsibility to attempt to remove the imperfections of our society. This book started with an awareness of the importance of the mental nurturing of our newborns from 0 to 5. These newborns grow up to become local leaders and national leaders. If we, as a society, start now to address the "mental nurturing" of our society by attempting to remove these examples of functional insanity, then we could change our society for the better.

CHAPTER 5

Functional Insanity: Gun Violence

Man is incapable of governing himself. The police force was created to maintain peace and order within the masses. As a society, it was agreed upon that this body was needed. The point I want to make is that we endorse the police as our protector, but this endorsement gives little real comfort to most of our citizens. As a result, most citizens feel that they need weapons, especially guns, to protect themselves. How does this relate to common sense, reason, logic, and practicality? We pay groups to protect us. We pay the Army, Navy, Marines, Air Force, Coast Guard, sheriff departments, police departments, marshals, and other agencies like the FBI, CIA, and so on. These departments and agencies are paid with tax money. So why do people feel that they must have guns in their homes for protection? Have you ever really thought about that? Are you willing to concur with me that we indeed have a problem with "mental nurturing" in this country? An average of approximately 40,000 US citizens dies from gun violence every year. If 40,000 soldiers died in one year during a war, people would be in the streets demanding that we stop the war. However, in contrast, we never look at gun sales in our country as something that needs to be curtailed. There are multiple nations that restrict or ban guns: China, India, Indonesia, Japan, Iran, Lebanon, Malaysia, Singapore, North Korea, Taiwan, Venezuela, Vietnam, and more. We have more guns than people in the United States.

We are largely a Judeo-Christian nation that values the commandment from God that clearly states "Thou shalt not kill." Would you agree that something is wrong with this picture when the current syndrome is for everyone to own a gun? The mental nurturing problem that is evident in our country is not being addressed by our political leaders and sadly neither by our Christian leaders. The adage that states "practice what you preach" is missing in pulpits across America. Our Christian churches contribute to the imperfections found within our masses. If we as a nation do not recognize and work on the mental nurturing of our society, we will not need to worry about global warming because we will surely self-destruct. Guns should not be sold to citizens.

In 2018, a man went into a Christian church and killed nine people with a gun, but not one Christian organization spoke out about stopping the sale of guns. Every day forces we hire to protect us suffer from gun violence get shot across the streets of our nation. Yet, few organizations have thought about taking the guns out of the hands of our citizenry to ensure the safety of those we hire to protect us. If the citizenry didn't have guns, the police could perform their jobs with a newfound proficiency. They could go into situations and be free of worry about being shot or inadvertently drawing their guns out of fear that a suspect had a gun.

Our nation is rapidly becoming functionally insane, yet we can't see it. Why do we go to church to ask God for protection but go to gun stores and stock up on guns to kill? Where is our faith in God? Are we depicting Jesus Christ in our actions? I pray that we will change our ways and come to the realization that we must work on removing the inhumane imperfections found in our society. We urgently need to initiate gun control with a direct intent to remove all guns from individual citizenry. Our future depends on all of us removing the things in our society that are ungodly and lead to self-destruction.

Politicians and clergy, you are the leaders that people follow. I challenge you to lead our people to mental sanity instead of letting them drift into functional insanity, Let me define:

Functional Insanity = is the inability to properly use common sense, reason, logic, and practicality.

People in this category do not know right from wrong nor what is good or bad, and they are lacking in discernment. They are not able to make good decisions for themselves. Functionally insane people are incapable of really thinking for themselves, so they follow other ideas and opinions. Most societies have traits of functional insanity. Millions of Americans are followers. Functional insanity is contagious. One individual can easily spread it to a group. Today, you hear about men and women killing their children. We hear about children killing their parents and children committing suicide. Through tv and movies we see stories that depicts normality yet pull off heinous crimes. Show like, Unsolved Mysteries, Ture Crime, Fatal Attraction, etc. are examples of this behavior. Unfortunately, nothing goes off in our brains that something is wrong with the minds of these people who commit shocking and senseless murders. Few people think that we have a mental nurturing problem in the United States. We often hear about these atrocities and pass it off as a sign of the times rather than consider that we should educate people concerning the importance of mental nurturing.

CHAPTER 6

Human Warning Signs

Weather has changed over the years. We recognize that. We even work together to form groups that study climate change. We have already made changes in society to address these changes. We have given the climate change a name, "Global Warming." Because of all the actions taken by global warming groups, and our politicians, coal mines have been shut down, cars have new emission standards, etc. However, we appear to be totally blind to the fact that human beings have changed in character and conduct over the years, much more than the weather has changed.

When I was born in 1943, there were no such things as burglar bars on doors and windows. Young girls who had a baby at a young age were an embarrassment to their families. Fathers of these young pregnant girls wanted the man who made his daughter pregnant to marry her. Any kind of crime was big news in the community. Murders were shocking. Over time, the conduct and character of America has changed drastically. Murder has become normalized, and younger girls are becoming pregnant with no thoughts of marriage. The character of our masses has changed much more than the weather has changed.

Functional Insanity: Racism
Racism has been a problem in our country since slavery. Racism is a problem because of ignorance. This ignorance keeps people from using common sense, reason, logic, and practically. There has been a racist mentality since slavery. I am not innocent. I hated white people at one time. I hated white people for many years because of something that happened in Mississippi when I was 13 years old. A white man tried to take my sister in the woods and rape her. He could have killed her. My mother was a domestic worker for some of the white people in the little town we lived in. She went to their homes and cooked for them, washed, and ironed their clothes, cleaned the houses, and did all the chores she was asked to do. Her employers knew our family. My sister often babysat for the white family that employed my mother.

One night, my sister went to babysit for this family. After the family came back home, they sent her home by a trusted a friend of theirs that live past our home. She got into the truck with a white man. He did not drop her off at our house. He sped up while driving her further away from our house. My sister was terrified because he would not let her out. She began to panic because she did not know what he was about to do. She jumped out of the fast-moving truck, and by the grace of God, she was able to crawl off into the dark. She hid. He turned around and tried to find her. She finally made it back to our house. I will never forget that night when the whole house was awakened by the pounding on our door. My parents opened the door and let her in. We were all shocked at first, and then we got angry. I was very proud of my dad that night because he quickly put on his pants and told me to put my clothes on. He grabbed the shotgun he used for hunting wild game, and he gave me the smaller gun. He put shells in his pocket. We walked two miles down the street to where the people she was babysitting lived. We knocked angrily on the door and told the people she babysat for what happened. The man and woman we talked to told us how sorry they were and that they would see that the man who kidnapped my sister would pay for what he had done.

Where I was born, everyone knew each other in town. White and black people knew each other. My family was well liked and respected by whites, but back then, if you were black, you had a place in society, and that place was not equal to whites. This was in the middle or late 50s. The man they let bring my sister home was a schoolteacher at the white high school. (Schools had not been integrated then.) We did not know the white man who did this to my sister. The price he had to pay for trying to rape my sister was to be fired from his job as a teacher in the local school. There were no formal charges, no arrest, no jail or prison time. That was the white man's justice in Mississippi.

If my sister's trauma was not enough, a young black teenager named Emmitt Till was brutally and horrendously murdered because he allegedly whistled at a young white female clerk at a grocery store. This happened to Emmitt in August of 1955. This was only a few months after, the schoolteacher tried rape my sister. The way Emmitt Till was murdered, coupled with what happened to my sister and the penalty the perpetrator had to pay, gave me what I thought at the time a reason to hate all white people. So, from 1955 until 1989, I literally embraced a deep-seated hatred for all white people. I believe that I had always seen hate as something that made people crazy without them knowing it.

I used to see white people come pick my mother up in their cars or trucks, and my mother would always get into the back seats. These were white people that loved my mother's cooking more than the domestic work she did for them. My family was looked upon with favor by most of the white people in town because of my mother's work ethic and culinary ability. Yet, she was not good enough to sit in the front seat of a white person's car. She was never invited to sit at the table to eat with them. As I gained knowledge of these facts, I said to myself at an early age, "that's crazy." Hatred and racism had those Mississippi white people's minds messed up. The person who literally cooked the food that they were consuming was not good enough to sit in the front seat of their car nor worthy to sit at the same table. Functional insanity existed long ago, but now it has exacerbated to the point of making our nations masses be grossly affected to a very dangerous level.

CHAPTER 7

My Experience

I had a spiritual experience in 1989, while in a cell at the Louisiana State Penitentiary. I was in the worst punishment camp called "Camp J." I was in and out of the dungeon for the first ten years of my incarceration. The dungeon is a disciplinary building with cells to penalize inmates. However, I would always take my Bible with me. I knew I would need something to read. Praying and reading the Bible provided nourishment for me, and it turned into wisdom. These trips to the dungeons provided me the space I needed to fulfill my parental responsibility. I wrote my four children frequently because God revealed to me that if I nurtured my children's minds, they would make it without my physical presence. I wrote my children letters from my heart. I lived life with them through the written page. By the grace of God, all my children are blessed.

Now back to my Damascus Road experience. I had just finished reading in the book of Psalms, and I got up and went to the bars of my cell to peep as far as I could down the hall. I saw a vision of a row of lights lined up and down the hall. I was in a state of amazement because I knew that what I was seeing couldn't be real. I made a concentrated effort to look again, and the two bright lights were still there. I left the bars and sat back down, and the lights stayed on for about a minute longer. I could see the hall get dark again. My mind was in a quagmire over the row of lights because it was impossible. I asked God what the lights meant. After I prayed, I laid silently, waiting for God to show me the meaning of the lights. God began to show me the hate I had in me. God directed my mind to get rid of the hate I had for white people. I was hesitant to latch on to that message until God nurtured my thinking to change through common sense, reason, logic, and practicality. Many of the trips I made to the dungeon were long stays, and during some of that time, I read books of all genres of self-help books, civil rights books, and autobiographies most about blacks. The knowledge I gained about the underground railroad was the most compelling reading that opened my mind to how wrong I was to embrace hate for all white people, or any people for that matter. Through common sense that God gave me, I recognized that Harriet Tubman could not have succeeded in organizing the underground railroad without the aid of white people. White people were the ones who the slaves were taken to so that they could gain freedom. I read about John Brown and his sons fighting to the death to free slaves. I also read about the author of the song "Amazing Grace", John Newton, who was once the owner of a slave ship and the conversion of John Newton. God revealed to me how wrong I was to hate. Hate was not how God wanted me to live in the world. God instructed me to use common sense, reason, logic, and practicality when I made decisions, especially as it related to race. No human being should hate because it neither pleases God nor his son Jesus. Those who hate will not be able to use proper discernment in life because hate nor racism has any redeeming qualities.

God asked me, "Does it make sense to hate another human just because they are not the same skin color as you?" Can you find logic or reason in such thinking of hate or racism? God also revealed to me that I could never follow the example of Jesus because if I hate others, I cannot help others to do God's will. Racism and hate remove the ability to reach out in love to others. I never thought that I would ever stop hating white people for what happened to my sister and Emmitt Till, but on that night in a cell by myself, God visited me. He revealed his truth to me. Hate nor racism will never enter my heart again because by God's wisdom I know how to properly use common sense, reason, logic, and practicality. After that experience, my life in prison changed. I went from being the most incorrigible prisoner in the Angola Louisiana State Penitentiary to being a model prisoner. The hate and racism within our society right now will destroy us if we refuse to see each other as humans who are all equal. We must live together and refuse to hate one another because of the color of skin. Could you hate children of different races? And if you do, and I pray not, ask yourself why? Why do you hate someone that did not ask to be born? No one born has a choice in the matter. If you hate a baby or any young children simply because of their skin color, you are a sick person who needs help.

I overcame thoughts of hate and racism in a prison cell. I wonder if I had not been incarcerated if I would have taken the time to build a relationship with God or experienced the spiritual phenomenon that took place in the hall of that prison dungeon. I think many people in the world do not take the time to isolate themselves from the distractions of the world. Consequently, quiet thoughts about racism and hate never to enter their minds. It is difficult for many people to really take inventory of their intrinsic thoughts and values. Thinking independently is something that is not taught in our schools or in most homes.

As a result, our children do not experience quiet moments to connect with God through prayer or experience the quiet atmosphere of thinking. How can our children be properly mentally nourished when they are never introduced to any power greater than themselves? For years, society has not effectively taught enough against racism and hate. If our young children were taught to love all humanity regardless of race, creed, or color, then hate and racism would have no space to exist.

Our churches should teach against hate and racism with a specific design in the biblical instructions to penetrate the consciousness our young people. If parents would teach their children that hate and racism are wrong, then society would eradicate hate and racism over time. Parents are a child's first teacher. Churches should be challenged to teach everyone that hate, and racism are not godly. Proper mental nurturing to our young is the only way we can remove the imperfections that negatively affect the conduct and character of our nation. In the process of doing 31 years in prison, by God's grace, I overcame hate and racism. I heard about many things that were going on in society, and I always wondered why these things were allowed to happen in a free society of intelligent people.

You can make a difference.

I have mentioned functional insanity many times in this book. There are a few more things that society knows but never really thinks about critically. Regarding, how much power and important the individual self is to society. I want to talk about one main reason why things are getting worse. It starts with you. I want you to look at yourself and be honest. Please do not ever think, "I'm just one person, and I can't do anything about it."

Everything that exists in this world today, exists from an individual's mind. According to the Bible, the thought of creating Earth came from a thought of God, and from that thought Earth was formed. God thought it. God spoke it. God made it. Thinking leads to action. You are self-prophesying, when you believe that you cannot do anything because you are just one person. Disbelief kills the will to try. If you think you cannot make a difference because you are one person, then you will not do anything. When you see things, you don't like, ask yourself, "What can I do about this?" Inaction causes things to get worse over time. You cannot always depend on everyone else to make the changes you want to experience.

CHAPTER 8

Functional Insanity: Parenting

A lack of mental nurturing results in functional insanity. Do you know why a law was created to stop parents from using corporal punishment on their children? The real reason was that society recognized a negative mental nurturing in our children. Many parents were too immature to raise a child, and this resulted in a lack of mental nurturing. These parents allowed little children to make them angry enough to abuse them. Too many ignorant people in society think that the government went too far in enacting this law, yet they never considered why. The law was created because someone saw that innocent children were victims of brutalization by an adult who didn't know how to parent. I agree with the law that forbids parents from beating their children. I agree with the law because I firmly believe, you can't beat sense into any human's head.

I will use my own experience to give credence to this statement. My mother used corporal punishment on me and my brothers and sisters. She made me go get the switch that she was going to whip me with. That's how Mississippi parents would do their children back then. They would make you go get the switch off a tree limb or shrub in the yard around the house. I would try to find the smallest switch I could. The pain from the switch would not make me behave. I would still engage in the bad behavior and made certain that I would not get caught. I became sneaky. If one of my brothers or sisters was around, and I thought one of them would tell my mom, I simply would not do it. However, the first chance I got, I did it. So, in essence, sense was not beat into me because I kept doing the wrong thing. Corporal punishment made me sneaky instead of righteous. Parents should stop feeling like the government did them a disservice by outlawing corporal punishment.

The things my mother talked to me about before whipping me were vital for me, assuming I would never do it again. My mom told me why she was whipping me. She told me about the consequences for what I did and how it could hurt me or someone else. My mom didn't just grab a switch and whip me out of her instant anger about what I did. She persuaded me that what I did was wrong by talking to me before and after she used the switch on me. She would always ask me questions. For example, she would ask, "Do you understand?" or "Do you think that was right what you did?" or "Do you feel bad for what you did?" After she whipped me, she would ask me, "Are you going to do that again?" My mom usually talked to me about what I had done before and after disciplining me. I now know that she was talking common sense, reason, logic, and practicality into my mind. I love her spirit for talking to me.

Today, you see parents who do not know how to raise their children. Little children now curse long before they reach the age of five years old. Do you think this is acceptable? You see it, but you don't think you can do anything about it because you are just one person. As a result, you do not try to change anything. If we want to curtail the perpetual downward spiral our country, we need to stop teaching our children to be losers by our own inactivity. The positive development of our children is something that we have never paid enough attention to in our society. It is time to wake up!!

CHAPTER 9

Functional Insanity: Entertainment

Another imperfection that demands attention can be found in most of the things that entertain us. We have idols that we worship without knowing it. We have idolized the rich and famous. Sports stars, singers, and actors attain millions of worshippers. These fans display profound emotions toward these human idols. Some fans cry, others faint, and some jump for joy and display unbelievable passions for their star. Both young and old are guilty. Strangely, these entertainers do not offer their fans anything but a euphoric feeling.

Sports have become an idol. Riots have occurred when teams win and lose. Cars are turned over. Things are set on fire. Buildings are vandalized. Most of us watch this activity on the television from a safe place like our home. Have you ever just wondered what's going on in the minds of people that engage in this idol worship? These rebellious actions cannot be seen as a joyful reaction. This is another example of societal imperfection and functional insanity. This has become an acceptable form of lawlessness caused by idolatry. This euphoria has dulled man's ability to use common sense, reason, logic, and practicality. Yet, we see the behavior spoken of as normal.

We must all contribute to society in order to save it. I implore the famous entertainers to help humanity but not in an acrimonious way. I would not ask them to stop recording songs, but I would ask them to help society by changing the message found in the songs. Their music has a great influence on the human mind. Pay attention to the songs that are played on the radio. Repetition leads to familiarity. Music should have positive messages that encourage us to treat each other with dignity and respect. We all know that curse words and lewd talk are not good for the "mentally nurturing" of our children. This should be removed from songs that our young are exposed to. I would expect this plea to fall on deaf ears. Change is not easy. However, over time, it can become the norm if were willing to look inside of ourselves for the necessity of such change.

Majority rules. Change will only take place if the majority of the music entertainers buy into this concept. Keep the beat, but the messages must change. The world would be a better place if our music contained positive messages. I would ask the entertainers of today, "In your heart and soul, do you feel an obligation to better society and provide a positive influence?" Our movie industry is also negatively affecting the mental nurturing of our children. The movie industry may be more harmful to our society than any other form of entertainment. The most popular movies are based upon fiction and lack reality. The following are examples of blockbuster movies based in fiction: *Avengers*, *The Last Jedi*, *The Force Awakens*, *Avengers Infinity War*, *Harry Potter*, *Jurassic World*, *The Lion King*, *Black Panther*, and *The Incredibles*. I listed these top movies for a reason because I want you to see that none of the movies are based upon reality. We are perpetually infiltrating our American masses with violent fiction. This is what we keep pumping into the brains of our adults and children. There is an old saying that says, "Too much of anything is not good." For the proper mental nurturing of our country, it would be wise to put restrictions on movies. Why? Look at what's going on in our streets. What is leading our young people to engage in criminal activity, commit suicide, or kill others? Previously, our society thought it would be sufficient to rate a movie. People believed that this would solve the problem. We never considered the damage that movies could do to young, underdeveloped brains or the brains of adults that were never properly nurtured. You rarely hear of negative behavior patterns affiliated with watching movies.

Remember that earlier in this book, I expounded upon the importance of mental nurturing in the development of children ages 0 to 5. The foundational years of 0 to 5 prepares a human to be an independent thinker. Independent thinkers can discern fact from fiction. However, individuals that lack critical thinking skills often struggle with differentiating between the two. Proper parenting prepares the individual to discern fiction from truth. The mental nurturing of children is critical to the health of our society. Approximately 20 years ago, a movie about a college football team showed a scene where football players, from the winning team, laid down in the center of a heavily trafficked road to show how grand their huevos were. It was only a movie, but a few impressionable teenagers emulated the scene they saw in the movie, and one of the teenagers was killed by a car. Unfortunately, two more were badly hurt. The name of the movie was called *The Program* starring James Caan and Halle Berry. As a result of the deaths and injuries caused by the movie, that scene was removed from the movie. This is just one example that movies impact the brains of viewers. I would like to challenge film executives. You are preparing the industry to self-destruct if you keep making movies that are rife with negative messaging. You are filling the brains of society with insane events and actions. I will keep saying this: We have a mental nurturing problem in this nation, and it will not get better until we all work on it. I know many film executives and producers will claim that they have the freedom of speech to make these movies. In my opinion, freedom of speech needs to be amended. Anything that does harm to the masses, whether intended or not, should be scrutinized and changed. The first amendment is one of the most appealing aspects of democracy. However, when you put it under a microscope, you can see the germs running around in it. The first amendment can be exploited. People often use the first amendment to spread lies and engage in propaganda. Many of our citizens don't know the truth from a lie because of the exploitation of freedom of speech. We must do better, or we will self-destruct. The privilege of freedom of speech needs to be amended, and specific language needs to replace ambiguous mandates and allowances. No one should have a right to lie. A right that obviously does more harm than good needs to be curtailed. Anything that does more harm than good for our society needs to be removed.

I'm writing this entire book because God directs my path. Through the wisdom God gave me, I give to you.

Have you realized that our nation is suffering from a lack of proper mental nurturing? There's one thing God gave us total control over: the brain. No one can control your brain except for you.

The brain is what I call a marvelous machine. Most of us are unaware about how marvelous the brain is. All human actions start in the brain. Mental nurturing leads to critical thinking.

CHAPTER 10

Functional Insanity: Foster-care System

I want to address another imperfection that needs fixing. Many people in our society are pro-life advocates. It is an excellent and godly quality to want to see all of life live. I look into my heart and soul and asked God to give me an answer about pro-life advocacy. God revealed to me that I should be pro-life only if I would accept responsibility for new life. If I merely claim to be pro-life and do not take responsibility, then I am a hypocrite. Millions of people claim to be pro-life, yet there are more than 400,000 children in foster care homes. These children have no mom or dad to hold them in their arms or tuck them away at night with an occasional story. I also wonder how many little babies are born into dysfunctional homes.

Think about this. In some places, as high as 40% of children who were in foster care become homeless, and 25% of these children go in and out of prison. Up to 80% have significant mental health related problems. The truth is that many foster care children spend a life of hell here on earth. No human asks to be born, and every baby born deserves to at least have a chance to live a decent life. Fellow Christian brothers and sisters, have you ever thought about what happens to the new life that we insisted be brought into this world by women that did not want them? Who will take responsibility for this new life? Who will be responsible for this little child? I believe that many of our Christian brothers are sincere and innocent in wanting to make life sacred, but we make the mistake of seeing life from one perspective.

Many of those who come from foster homes commit suicide. Think about it! Who will claim responsibility for that? Foster care children often have a lack of self-esteem. Why? Society at large is not kind and welcoming to children from foster homes. I know our Creator would be pleased if we as Christians worked to better our foster homes. Christians have a responsibility to care for the orphans of society. Foster homes need a new design that ensures the mental nurturing of the child. Parenting classes are needed. We should treat foster care children the same as we do our own children. I pray that pro-life Christians will begin to display a remarkable compassion that leads to action toward laws being passed to protect children in the foster care system. We need to make the unwanted feel wanted. I would be remiss to overlook our homeless people. I cannot pass them up without having empathy and sympathy for them.

Functional Insanity: Homelessness
If you want to see the worst example of our society's failure to mentally nurture our masses, all you have to do is look at the homeless. No human being in their right mind would intentionally want to be homeless. Some may use their homelessness as a hustle, but even the ones who do that have a mental problem. We often pass up a homeless person and refuse to give them a dollar or two because

we think that they are lazy. If I see a homeless person begging and I have money to spare, I will give it to them. Most of the recipients of my donations are extremely thankful.

Have you ever wondered why homeless people drink a lot? I think it's because they do not like their reality. Therefore, they drink to escape their past and current pain. This can be traced back to a lack of mental nurturing. Many of our homeless have never had the opportunity to thrive in society. Their only option is begging. A person cannot get a good paying job without an education. We see homeless people everywhere. Have you ever taken the time to ask what led to their homelessness? I implore you to have love and compassion for our homeless population. Homelessness is a product of our imperfect society.

The homeless population needs to experience the love and grace found in Jesus and find their identify in him. Homeless people need hope and faith in something greater than man. Believing in something greater than man gives a person a new hope in life and feel a greater sense worth. Are you willing to engage in dialogue with a homeless person? We may give them a fleeting dollar. We might embrace a quick thought of sympathy or empathy toward them. However, after that small act of philanthropy, we often forget the homeless person we encountered. Your gift to the homeless depicts your humaneness and concern for humanity. It is a noble gesture.

Our society has placed homeless people at the bottom. The reaction of the upper classes towards the homeless is often one of reticent scorn. Do we treat the homeless as people who have worth? Do we treat the homeless as men and women who are created in the image of God? Do we really care about the homeless? If we happen to ask them how they are doing, do we really want them to give us an answer?

My prayer is that in the future we can eliminate homelessness altogether. The most prosperous nation on earth should not have homelessness. It is ironic that our congressmen can only talk about working to help the middle class. The lower class and homeless class woes are the least of the concern of our elected officials. We need to build more homeless shelters, and we need to make the homeless shelters look more like a home rather than a human warehouse. All the homeless shelters should be places that depict good morals, principals, and values. They should also embrace an atmosphere of good manners and congeniality.

CHAPTER 11

My Encounter with God

I now ask you to look at the country I love and its people whom I love. Here's another experience with God in the dungeon. This encounter happened while I was locked up in maximum security." Inmates are given a little freedom while in the dungeon. I was given the liberty to go out on the yard for one hour and either sit or walk during that time. I usually walked or jogged for that precious hour of liberty; however, on this day, I decided to walk. As I circled the cell block dungeon, this walk became a revelation from God, and resulted in wisdom. As I started taking steps around the yard, an awesomeness came over me that made me see God's splendor. I began to see a new hue that entered my eyesight. I gained a new perspective about everything I saw. Things came alive. I saw the green grass and flowers like never before. The green grass was greener; the colors of the flowers took on a new and radiant splendor. The different colors of the flowers were more beautiful than I had ever seen. This was a bizarre revelation to me, but it was just the beginning. As walked down the fence, I saw a bird that was absolutely the prettiest bird I had ever seen. This bird was not a common bird because its feathers had at least 5 different colors in perfect order. I have seen many birds while being let out to walk the fence, but none of the previous birds could even come close to grabbing my attention like the one I saw on this day. As I kept sauntering around the yard, I noticed my peers walking from the cellblocks in a line, with prison guards on horseback, going to work the fields. The guards had guns on their shoulders, which was not a new scene for me at all.

However, this time I had a different perspective about what I saw. It was like I was looking at a video as opposed to viewing it with my eyes. God revealed to me that what I was seeing was in fact a video I had already recorded. Your brain records everything the eyes see. You could also call it a scene out of the movie of your life. That day the red was redder, the blue colors were bluer, the green was greener, and every single other color I saw looked brighter. I've looked at the sky since I was a little kid, but I had never seen the sky like I saw it on this day. On this day, I saw God's artwork; we call them clouds. I had seen the shapes and configurations of clouds all my life, but I never entertained the thought that the clouds we see as God's artwork until that day when I felt the presence of God. As I was heading inside, a gentle breeze hit me. I went back to my cell and was overwhelmed at what I had just experienced. After taking a shower and settling in my cell, God revealed to me that man was not recognizing his presence all around them. God revealed to me that the bird that I saw on the fence had been there before. The grass had always been that green. The sun shone bright, and the gentle breeze provided a respite from the heat. God revealed to me that because I had been praying to him for wisdom, knowledge, strength, courage, and love he would introduce himself to me. Even when I was in my sin, I prayed to God. God came to me while I was in prison.

I now know that God has been with me my whole life. God showed me that he provides for me every day. We take for granted that we should be able to see, hear, walk, talk, and taste. I read in a book named *Think and Grow Rich* that we as humans are born rich. The book asked the question about how much money you would give up to get your sight back if you were blind. He applied the same question to all the other senses. The message he gave by those comparisons compelled me to concur with his statement that "we are born rich." It's true we are born rich, but we take it for granted or else we would thank God every day. We should look for things to be thankful and happy about. Many of us look for things to complain about and in essence make our own lives miserable. Next time you feel depressed, think about the riches that God gave you at no cost. I've seen people who did not have the uses of all their fine senses radiate a spirit of thankfulness and joy. It is all about perspective. If you struggle with being grateful, then pray to God, and ask God to show you the way. My entire perspective about God changed after I was introduced to him. I now see things differently.

CHAPTER 12

Functional Insanity: Our Youth

I want to tell you about some of the things that I see. Recently, I had the occasion to talk with two teenage girls. I have a habit of engaging dialogue with our young girls and boys because I need to know how they think if I am going to help them. I've tried to encourage older men like me to dialogue with our young boys and girls. I have not achieved much success. Older adults normally tell me that they are not going to engage in dialogue with youth because they say, "It won't do no good." They often tell me that they tried in the past, but the youth would not listen. I think that some of the old men I tried to recruit were not capable of engaging in dialogue with our young people. It could also be that the young people were offended in some way, and as a result, the older adults never tried to talk to them again. Our young people are missing the commonsense dialogue that we older men use to pass on to our young ones. Our youth are not learning how to use common sense, reason, logic, or practicality.

Years ago, common sense, reason, logic, and practicality was taught to our young by the television and radio. Most of the T.V. programs promoted good morals, respect, love, and concern for fellow man. This even applied to the sitcoms that featured animals as stars. In these T.V. shows, right won over wrong and blasphemous words were not allowed. One prime example of an hour-long weekly sitcom was the *Little House on the Prairie*. This is my favorite T.V. show. This show teaches many positive values. We need shows like this today. Our children perpetually suffer from a lack of knowledge. Will you help me in trying to solve this problem? Are you willing to have a dialogue with young people and pass on to them commonsense?

Here in this great nation, we need to be reminded that we are all on the same team. The team concept is all for one and one for all. Teamwork leads to strength and not weakness. Sports fans and entertainment fans embrace this team concept. For example, just observe the clapping, high fives, shouts, and yells that take place after a home team scores a touchdown. All races are united in the stadium. White, black, Asian, Hispanic, etc. are cheering for the same team in unity. This is a beautiful sight. We are one. During this home win euphoria, race does not matter. When the home team wins, people of different races, creeds and colors all have fun. Unfortunately, the next day the beauty of the day before is gone. It vanishes as if it was a long mirage.

America, wakeup. The country you live in is the strongest nation in this world. The conduct and character of its people made it that way. America's team (USA) is getting weaker with every passing day. We have a elements in society that are trying very diligently to try to break the sovereignty of this nation. Men with no vision that think things will turn out good if we engage in a civil war. The most destructive emotion that humans can experience is hate. It is impossible for you to use common sense, reason, logic, nor practicality while you hate others. Hate strips people of their humanity. Hate destroys communication. Communication is essential in the advancement of anything. If I hate Mexicans because of the color of their skin, then the hate in me will influence me not to talk to Mexican people. If you hate, you cannot relate to others. You cannot be a team player with American society because there's no solidarity in hate. Hate is splitting up America.

I have question for the reader. Are you happy that we are not at war? Do you enjoy having freedom? Do you want America to continue to be the model nation for the world? I know I do, and I think other sane people would feel the same way. There is a real threat going on right now in this country. The consequence of hate is destruction. We can never be a team if hate is present.

The mental nurturing of our young and old must be one that teaches humans not to hate. Hate is a learned negative emotion. In the process of learning, humans need to be taught not to hate and be instructed on the reasons why they should not hate. Parents have not done a good job of teaching our young and old not to hate. We as a people can change that with proper action. We must convince the masses that hate does harm to the brain. They must be taught to use their common sense, reason, logic, and practicality. Human beings need to be taught these things so that they can have proper discernment. I will say it repeatedly in this book: we must start with humans when they are born. Thus, 0 to 5 years of age is crucial to human development.

Parents are the children's first teacher. Society needs to recognize that and prepare future mothers and fathers with the knowledge they need to parent effectively. It is not an easy task to teach a child to not hate. Children must understand the negative things that hate does to their brain. Children need to be told at an early age that hate could cause relational problems and that hate is the wrong way to feel about people you don't know or have ever met. I believe that hate would decrease in America if we would have open dialogue with our children. Our world could be a better place.

I want to tell you how to teach your children against hate. You simply tell them the truth about the negative effects of hate. Hate makes you brain think destructive things. Hate causes a person to be upset with others and hate cuts of your ability to communicate. Hate can cause physical and mental harm in your brain. Hateful thoughts towards others leads to high blood pressure. Hate could lead to criminal acts of violence, and cause one person to kill another person.

The black race of Americans are victims of being hated by white people, who have never met them. This is because of the rhetoric that the news media puts out. However, the rhetoric is written in a particular way to imply that blacks are a burden on the economy, perpetrators of all the criminal endeavors, and just basically bad citizens. There is a myth out there that says welfare is a burden on the economy, and Congress under the conservative party wants to cut what meager allotment they get now. To go along with the first myth, they also say that blacks are just lazy and don't want to work, so why should they have to pay taxes to help people who just don't want to work? Blacks are also blamed for crime in America.

The average working white men and women in society could easily agree with all the bad things said about black people being a burden on the economy, if they are not familiar with the real reasons. This kind of rhetoric shouts that blacks get free money from hardworking people. Many whites who hear this rhetoric believe what they are hearing is true, and this thinking opens the door to hate. This leads to hate without evidence. Most welfare recipients never heard of embezzlement, subterfuge, nor fraudulent endeavor. However, these are the main criminal activity used to drain the economy.

For those who don't know, I am about to give you a few facts. Your number one enemy, when it comes to being a burden on the budget, is not welfare recipients. It is men who attain government contracts for infrastructure work and any other contractual work for the government. If you are really concerned about wasteful spending, don't look at the pittance that may be found in welfare wasteful spending. Instead, look at the money that is wasted in government contracts with the private sector. Also, look at the defense budget. The defense budget is one third of our annual national budget. I can see maintaining our military salaries and equipment, but not the constant building of more machines year after year when there is no active war. Over seven hundred billion dollars is spent on the defense of our nation. Do you think you could find some wasteful spending within that $700 billion? Welfare and food stamp budgets is less than 1% in comparison to defense spending in times of peace.

Politicians have an open check to spend your money. You hear about how they spend taxpayer's money living in mansions, spending time in luxurious hotels, buying gifts, and flying airplanes all over the place. I guess it's okay to use taxpayer's money if you work for the government. White collar crime has been allowed for too long without being subject to equivalent judicial scrutiny. The crimes that you hear about or see on T.V. does not include all the crime that's going on in that day. It does not show the crimes that fall under these names: embezzlement, subterfuge, and fraudulent circumvention. You only hear about these crimes when an important person is being convicted; however, with every passing second, minute, hour, and day, millions of dollars are being deleted from the national budget by white collar criminals. Please don't hate people once you know the real facts. Blacks are not the problem with our national budget. The problem is the greed of government contractors and exploitation of governmental funds that is executed by greedy politicians.

Let's talk about the social disadvantage of blacks in our communities.. I want to say that what I'm about to write does not come from reading books nor studying in a school setting. I speak as someone who has experience. To my white brothers and sisters, white people have little to fear from black crimes. Our own black people are living under unsafe living conditions. They live on dangerous streets. Many law-abiding citizens are afraid in their own neighborhoods. Can any of you say that you are afraid that you will be attacked by a black person on your street? Some people who want to destroy America will play up the crimes you see on the news to create a fear in you that blacks will harm you. Hate and fear are twins. If you have one you will most likely develop the other.

I'm going to try and explain to people that have a negative opinion about blacks. If you have never been a poor black that lives in an impoverished area, then you cannot possibly know how impoverished people feel nor why they act as they do. There is a lot of crime in black neighborhoods because most people living in impoverished neighborhoods have less proper education. For as many years that I can remember, statistics have proven that jails and prisons are full of men and women who never finished school. Statistics also show that schools have gotten worse every year in conduct and character. Do you see groups forming in the streets to demand that we fix our public schools? Why? The reason why is because something is hindering your brain from seeing our public schools as something to be alarmed about. Impoverished black families cannot afford to send their children to private school or some other school that you must pay for. Public schools are allowed to be bad because nobody has taken a stand demanding that our government fix our public schools.

Someone must have the wisdom to realize that we have a mental nurturing problem in American society. We need to fix it. One sure way we can all fix it, and that is to stop hating others because of the color of their skin.

CHAPTER 13

Functional Insanity: Professionals

I want to expound on social classes for a moment. First, I want to congratulate you who have achieved success in life. Secondly, you may be unaware to the realities around you. I implore the attention of all professionals such as doctors, lawyers, engineers, and department heads. Professionals are advised to look at the "man in the mirror" in regard to being a role model for our youth.

I went to a grocery store, during a weekday, that is located near a high school for troubled students. Students from the school would frequently come to the grocery store. On this day, I saw two girls approaching the basket area where I was. I stopped them. I asked them, "What are you all going to be doing 5 years from now?" The most aggressive one of the two turned around, started twerking and said, "I want to be a stripper". Soon after her friend stated she wanted to be a stripper also. These two young girls in high school, both were black, were contemplating a career as strippers as opposed to being doctors, engineers, scientists, lawyers, or business owners. When they finished answering my question, I went a little further and asked them why they chose that as a career, and to my surprise, they came with another quick response. Their response revealed that this was not them being sarcastic. They were serious.

They wanted to be strippers. The aggressive girl said, "They make a lot of money and it ain't no hard work." She went on to explain that it was a "cool job that don't tie you down." They enthusiastically talked about becoming strippers. I shed a tear that night because I thought about those two young girls. Society has allowed these two high school girls to reach this point. Society has allowed those two high school girls to be robbed positive self-image and self-esteem. They do not see their worth. Stripping was the future for these young girls.

Professionals, please wake up because we need your help. These two girls had no apparent role models to emulate other than other strippers. Why is this? Most of you professionals live in a gated community, or a plush neighborhood that has a professional guard providing protection. You have earned the right to live like you do, but what you fail to be aware of is how your success has allowed you to ignore segments of society. You may feel like you do not want to get involved in impoverished neighborhoods. Some of you probably have foundations or charity organizations that you give to. That's a good gesture, but you could set an example to our young people by being accessible and visible.

Many years ago, our children had role models that lived in big pretty houses and had a couple of nice cars. I grew up wanting to know who lived in those big houses and drove those fancy cars. I wanted to know what kind of job he or she had to afford such niceties. Schoolteachers used to get paid adequately in those days, when I was a young boy. School teachers owned big houses and had nice cars in the drive. The schoolteacher was my role model. I wanted to be like the schoolteacher because I liked his example.

He had nice things and was respected by others. Our young people have no nice homes to dream about because most professionals have moved out to some gated community or some plush neighborhood.

I implore professionals to step up and set an example. Be a hero to our youth. Our youth need to see you driving nice cars and owning big houses. Our young need positive role models. Our young boys and girls need role models who are professionals. Most professionals are good Americans. We need professionals to step up and become an image of success to our young. Professionals must be more visible in our communities and schools. This can be done by holding seminars, fairs, and exhibition in these areas. Since many professionals don't live in neighborhoods, they grew up in. This could motivate our children to succeed.

Most professional, are set for life regarding respect, income, and a comfortable lifestyle. For these individuals, it is easy to look at the things that go on and not be overly concerned about it. Out of sight and out of mind. Look at our society! You can make a difference. How many times have you heard or saw something on television and said to yourself, "That's crazy!" The thought of something being crazy was brought to your mind by the common-sense part of your brain. What you call "crazy" is in essence crazy in regard to how normal citizens are supposed to act. I am sure that you say or think something is "crazy" quite often if you are abreast with what is going on in America from day to day.

The lack of mental nurturing in our society is leading the masses to become functionally insane. I spoke about functional insanity in an earlier chapter. Remember, we have a mental nurturing problem in America. There are human warning signs all around us. We won't need to worry about global warming if the conduct and character of our society continues to decline. If you truly love mankind and want America to remain a sovereign nation, then you need to do your part to keep it that way. When you have spare time, go into these neighborhoods. Utilize the public schools to set up programs and workshops that allows our children to talk to successful people. This allows them to interact with professional for them to be role models emulate. We can restore civility in America, if we cast a vision of success for our children and encourage them to seek common sense, reason, logic, and practicality. This would curtail the functional insanity that is increasing with every passing day.

I believe America is the greatest nation on earth. However, I also believe that we are slipping into an unknown realm of functional insanity, and we must do something to curtail the inevitable. The things that must never change are love, integrity, principals, morals, and human decency. Character, love, and human decency are what set the norms for most of the masses. By God's grace, integrity is still in most of our societal masses. It is urgent that we gain back the love, integrity, morals, human decency, and values that made us the greatest nation on earth. God has provided us grace to see if we heed the warning. We desperately need our professionals in this fight.

So, 0 to 5 is where we begin the process, and then, we take it beyond. We need to take out the societal imperfections and replace them with positive ideas and thoughts. Society has not concentrated on how important it is to make sure that young and older parents know how to mentally nurture little innocent ones.

CHAPTER 14

Until we realize that here in America, we have a mental nurturing problem, we will keep thinking that all we need to do is hire more police, create more laws, and build more jails. Instead of locking people up for crimes, it is better to remove the ideas, thoughts, and other reasons that lead to criminal behavior. I will say this again, everything that happens now or that has ever happened first takes place in the mind. This is undeniable, so our common sense should tell us that we need to work on the source of the problem. Just like global warming advocates work on taking pollutants out of the air because these pollutants damage the ecosystem systems we live in, we also need to supply the very same concern for the ecosystem to our current society. People learn to adapt to the atmosphere they live in.

We are close to normalizing death in our culture—Not only with COVID-19 but also death in our streets. Remember that over 40,000 Americans die from gun violence every year, and a many of them are dying from suicide. Yet, a bell has not gone off in our heads that we urgently need to get guns out of the hands of everyone but our police and military. They are the ones WHO we pay to protect us. We would not need guns at all if our faith was strong in

God. We profess to be Christians but refuse to obey the teaching of Jesus and the doctrines found in the Holy Bible.

Functional Insanity: The Church

I've spoken extensively about hate and its offspring, fear. As Christians, we can do something now. Hate would diminish from our masses if churches began to integrate. There should be no such designation of the black church or the white church; we should all be willing and eager to attend any church where the word of God is taught. God is not pleased with the way man has made a bureaucracy out of the Christian church. We need the Christian church now more than ever to get rid of hate, fear and, most importantly, to hold the moral fiber of this great nation together. As men of God, we are failing to lead our young minds in the proper mental nurturing God wants us to. Our churches have become too secular and materialistic in design. Believe it or not, many people who need to hear the word of God do not get it because they do not have the money to pay tithes in the church. People in the congregation are looking at those who can't pay. As result, people simply do not go to church. I am not attacking the church but trying to help it to heal our society. However, God does not want us to ignore things that keep people from hearing and adhering to his word.

Man's law has replaced the Holy Spirit's free reign over the church. In today's world, a man or woman does not have to be called by God to preach, but he does have to pass man's test in finishing a Bible college to be allowed to take a pulpit in our churches. We saw a need to teach man to teach about God, but we haven't had the wisdom to teach parents how to teach their children. If our churches must have a bureaucracy, then this bureaucracy needs to curtail the individual pastors from accepting tithes as a criterion for membership. I am not a Catholic, but I like the way that the church handles tithing. You never see priest driving big fancy cars or living a lavish lifestyle suited for the rich and famous.

The church and state are supposed to be separated as designated by the constitution, but this is not the case in America. The church plays a huge role in our political arena. Man's interpretation of scriptures becomes ambiguous to fit certain political ideologies. God is not pleased with the way man has allowed this. Many churches are exploiting its members. God sent us a plague and a trial. COVID-19 was the plague, and the election was the trial. God has shown us grace and mercy with the plague, but the trial is only partially done. We must get rid of the hate that brought on the trial. The church bureaucracy and all its ministers need to start today to preach against hate or else you will not please God. Failure to please God, and to do his will leads to the self-destruction. The church and all denominations must stop demanding tithes so that people feel comfortable to come to church. Why can't pastors and ministers work regular jobs and preach God's word? Why can't preachers be paid regular salaries and the tithes that are taken up go to needy people within the congregation?

Let's be real and speak truth. I will reiterate that we need our churches to carry God's message of love and not hate. The church should remind people that there is a greater power, who when asked could strengthen the moral fibers of this nation.

I know that change is hard for some people to welcome, especially when it comes to customs and tradition, but for the good of all mankind, we must remove the things that are slowly bringing us to destruction.

To all the 217 various Christian denominations, I beseech you to preach the truth to your congregations. God has blessed you with the power of persuasion over men and women. Use this power to save our nation from self-destruction. Tell your flocks to not hate. Persuade them not to hate by using common sense, logic, reason, and practicality in your dialogue with them. You must tell them all the negative consequences that hate brings to ourselves and our fellow man. Hate has no positive manifestations.

CONCLUSION

I pray that this God inspired message is adhered to for the truth revealed to all who read this book.

Look at the changes that has taken place in our American society for the last 50 years, and honestly judge what has changed the most, the weather or the human behavior in man.

I sat in prison and watched the change in American society for 31 years continuous years, and I wondered how and why our American society allowed the changes to take place.

I too was going through a change in conduct and characters simultaneously just like the weather and the American society.

Throughout my change God was my guide. God bestowed wisdom into my countenance. This book is God's manifestation.

We are God's people, I gave you his message, and I pray that you will find the truth within the message God gave me to give to you.

I told you about your individuality, and that you can make a difference, and I encouraged you to never think that because you are only one person that you can't do something to make a difference about matters you see or hear about.

Things that you do not like or think is wrong do something about it. There are angles that you can take to do something about whatever.

Here are some people things that you can do: you can talk to others about it, or you can write to other people about it, or you can join a group of others who feel like you do about, or work as an individual to make a difference. The worst thing you can do is to do nothing.

This book was written by one man, in spite of years of incarceration, who never embraces the thought of " because I'm only one person I can do nothing."